Count the Cost

Jonathan Steadfast

COUNT THE COST.

AN ADDRESS TO THE PEOPLE of CONNECTICUT,
ON SUNDRY POLITICAL SUBJECTS,

AND

PARTICULARLY ON THE PROPOSITION FOR A NEW
CONSTITUTION.

BY

JONATHAN STEADFAST

1804

"However combinations or associations of the above description may now and then answer popular ends, they are likely in the course of time and things to become potent engines, by which cunning ambitions and unprincipled men will be enabled to subvert the power of the people, and to usurp to themselves, the reins of government, destroying afterwards the very engines which have lifted them to unjust dominion. "

WASHINGTON'S FAREWELL ADDRESS.

AN ADDRESS TO THE PEOPLE OF CONNECTICUT.

"FOR which of you intending to build a tower sitteth not down first and counteth the cost? "

Count the Cost

An interesting question is here asked by the direction of infinite wisdom. This question contains the following useful and important instruction: That no man or body of men should attempt the accomplishment of any great object without duly estimating the evils and benefits probably resulting from it. Such a rule of life and adopted and adhered to would have prevented many schemes and projects which have cost much, and which have been productive of nothing but the disgrace to their authors and misery to the human race—it would induce men to obey the dictates of experience rather than the dreams of enthusiasm, and would drive from the world a species of wisdom which is indeed folly.

An attempt is now making in this State to change the vital principles of our government, to remove from office all our present rulers, and to introduce a new order of things. To these innovations the people are invited, allured and exhorted. —To effect these objects no pains are spared—no exertions are omitted.

An important question here arises, viz. Would the accomplishment of the object be worth the cost? —An individual who neither holds an office nor seeks one— who can have nothing in view but the maintenance of that order of things which shall most effectually promote public and private happiness, and who has the same interest in the welfare of society as the great body of his fellow citizens, requests the dispassionate attention of the reader, while he considers this important subject. He will use no weapon but truth and truth will be regarded by all except those who love darkness rather than light.

To exhibit a correct view of the subject, it will be proper, first, to enquire into the present condition of Connecticut, and secondly, to examine the various plans or projects proposed for our adoption, and estimate the probably cost attending them. We can then in the third place form a just opinion of the propriety of the proposed changes.

The condition of Connecticut first claims our attention.

That our climate, soil and situation are such as to insure as much health, riches and prosperity as any people can rationally wish, seems not to be doubted. Our natural advantages do not indeed promise such an accumulation of wealth as might satisfy that avarice which like the horse leach is constantly crying give—give—they are such however as will in ordinary cases, ensure to industry an ample reward and this should satisfy a virtuous mind.

The diffusion of knowledge is greater than in any other part of the globe of equal dimensions. Such are the excellent provisions of our laws, and the virtuous habits of our citizens, that schools of instruction in all useful knowledge are to be found in every place where they are needed. There is no village in this State which will not attest to this fact. In various places also flourishing academies are supported, in which the higher branches of science are taught, and our College is at once our ornament and our pride. Religious instruction is also brought almost to every man's door, so that none can justly complain that they are denied the means of growing wiser and better. By the liberality of the benevolent private libraries are every where found which, with the other sources of information, evince the superiority of our condition to that of any other people, in the means of gaining valuable knowledge. To those, who with the writer, believe that ignorance is the parent of vice, and that the civilized is preferable to the savage state, our situation, in the above particulars, demands the gratitude of every heart.

Our constitution and government are perfectly free, and our laws are mild, equitable and just. To the truth of this position there is the most ample and unequivocal proof.

1. Those who seek to revolutionize the State declare this to be the nature of our government with few exceptions. —Such testimony cannot be doubted—it is the testimony of a man against himself. Ask your neighbour to point you to the evils under which he labours—ask him to name the man who is oppressed except by his vices or his follies, and if he be honest, he will tell you that there is no such man—if he be dishonest, his silence will be proof in point.

2. Strangers who reside here a sufficient time to learn our laws, universally concur in their declarations on this subject. They will ask, with surprize, why the people of Connecticut should complain? They see every man indulged in worshiping God as he pleases, and they see

many indulged in neglecting his worship entirely—They see men every where enjoying the liberty of doing what is right—and such liberty they rightly decide is the perfection of freedom.

3. The experience of a century and a half, affords irresistible proof on this subject. During this long period convulsions have shaken many parts of the earth, and there has been a mighty waste of human happiness. Empires and Kingdoms have been prostrated, and the sword hath been devouring without cessation. This state too hath been threatened— clouds have gathered and portended a dreadful desolation, but we have been defended, protected and saved. No essential changes in our government have ever taken place—formed by men who knew the important difference between liberty and licentiousness, it has been our shield— our strong tower—our secure fortress. —To the calls of our country we have ever been obedient—No state hath more cheerfully met danger—no state hath more readily or effectually resisted foreign aggression. Washington while living was a witness to this fact, and tho' dead he yet speaketh. While plots, insurrections and rebellions have distressed many states and nations, Connecticut hath enjoyed an internal peace and tranquility, which forcibly demonstrates the wisdom and equity of her Government. —Such a Government, administered by men of virtue and talents, has produced the most benign effects, and our prosperity is calculated to excite the warmest expressions of gratitude rather than the murmurs of disaffection.

4. Our Treasury exhibits the truth of these remarks. It is clear from the statement in the Appendix, to which every reader will advert with pleasure, that the people of Connecticut annually receive thirty seven thousand four hundred and fifty-five dollars and seventy six cents more from the Treasury than they pay into it by taxes and duties. —At the close of the late war such had been our exertions, we were encumbered with a debt of nearly two millions of dollars. Now that debt is paid and we have nearly that sum in advance. Where is the state which can justly boast of greater prosperity?

Notwithstanding this enviable situation a clamour is excited, the people are agitated, and discord, with its train of evils, is prevailing. Some of our citizens, in the height of political prosperity, are seeking to destroy an order of things which has prevailed an hundred and fifty years, and throw themselves into the arms of projectors and reformers. Is there nothing unaccountable in such conduct? Is there nothing calculated to excite indignation? My fellow citizens, shall any considerable portion of the people of Connecticut subject themselves to the reproach which rested on an ancient people? "The ox knoweth his owner and the ass his master's crib, but my people do not know, Israel doth not consider. "

Secondly. Let us examine some of the plans and projects proposed for our adoption and estimate the probably cost attending them.– Here we must speak with less certainty—What the present condition of Connecticut is we know—respecting its future destiny we can only judge by arguing from cause to effect. Why a man who regards the happiness of his fellow men, should attempt a change here, is too wonderful for an ordinary capacity. No prudent farmer ever pulled up a hill of corn, which was flourishing, to see if there was not a worm at the root.

One of these projects is the repeal of all laws for the support of religious institutions. The language of those who favor the measure is, that religion will take care of itself—that no external aid is necessary—that all legislative interference is impious. Many, and it is believed by far the greater part, of those who make these declarations, intend to throw down all the barriers which christianity has erected against vice. They are obstinately determined to banish from the public mind all affection and veneration for the Clergy, and respect for the institutions of religion, and to reduce Connecticut to that condition which knows no distinction between "him who serveth God and him who serveth him not. " They wish to see a Republic without religion; and should they be gratified, the consequence would speedily be, a miserable race of men without virtue, walling in vice and ripening for a dreadful destruction. If infinite truth is to be credited, "God will pour out his indignation on the heathen who know him not. "

These reformers, under the specious pretext of exercising unbounded liberality in matters of religion, become intolerant to all who differ from them, charging the professors of christianity with breathing out a spirit of persecution, they become the most furious persecutors, and while they affect to possess great moderation and candor towards all denominations of Christians, they clearly evince that they would grant indulgence or protection to none. On the other hand a great majority of the people and the Legislature, insist that every man in the community who is able, should contribute, in some way, towards the support of the institutions of religion. No wish is entertained to legislate in matters of faith, or to establish one sect in preference to another. Our laws permit every man to worship God when, where, and in the manner most agreeable to his principles or to his inclination, and not the least restraint is imposed; all ideas of dictating to the conscience are discarded, and every man "sits under his own vine and fig tree. " Our laws only enforce the great principle abovementioned that the members of the community should contribute towards the support of these institutions, as means to promote the prosperity of the people in the same manner as they provide for the public accommodation, peace and happiness, by the maintenance of the roads and bridges, the organization of the militia, and the support of schools of instruction. Should objections be urged by any individuals that they cannot conscientiously contribute to the promotion of these objects, their objections would be disregarded. There is a class of men, very respectable for the sobriety of their habits, and their peaceful deportment, who always refuse to be taxed for military defence. No one doubts that in their opposition, they are conscientious, and yet few doubt the propriety of enforcing such taxes.

The principle now advocated is interwoven with all our laws and habits — it has existed from the first settlement of the State—it has produced much good—it ought not therefore to be abandoned without the utmost deliberation. The clamor against this principle, is the clamor of those who wish to see the State revolutionized—it is the clamor of those turbulent spirits which delight in confusion and which pull down and destroy with a dexterity which they never shew in building up. Let the sober citizens of Connecticut look at the authors of this clamor—Let them view such men as Abraham Bishop, and eye the path which they have trodden from their youth, and then ask their own hearts, if they are not under some apprehension, lest if they should enlist under such leaders and fight their cause, they may be found contending against the best interests of society, and "fighting against God. "

Another project zealously supported is that of Districting the State for the choice of Assistants, and Representatives in Congress. The only argument which is urged for the adoption of this measure with any plausibility, is that in the District elections the candidate would be better known. To this argument it may be replied, the State of Connecticut is so limited in its extent, information of all kinds is so generally diffused, and there is such a flood of newspapers that the characters of all the candidates for office may be thoroughly known by all who will bestow any attention to the subject. This State is scarcely more extensive than a single county in many other States, and the intercourse of the inhabitants of the various parts with each other is such that no evil can exist in our present mode of elections—But there are serious and weighty objections against District elections.

1. Such elections open wide the door for intrigue. —As this door, already too widely extended, the most alarming mischiefs enter— mischiefs which sap the foundations of an elective government by corrupting the minds of the freemen and this converting an election ground into a theatre on which is displayed the most vile and demoralizing practices. Let the reader satisfy himself as to the truth of this observation by examining the history of an election in the Southern States, where this mode alone is adopted. Let him learn that they candidates for office and his host of dependents and tools, are employed for weeks before and on the days of election, in the most infamous intrigues, and that falsehood and bribery are so much in fashion, and are so universally resorted to, that success invariably attends the most impudent and the most profligate, while the man of modesty and virtue, though possessing the fairest claims to promotion, is abashed, confounded and overwhelmed.

2ndly. The candidate when elected becomes the creature of the district and not the ruler of a State—He is and must be devoted to the interest of that portion of the community which has elected him, and their views and schemes must be patronized though they oppose the welfare of the whole.

3rdly. Such elections do not secure the best talents. If talents and worth are of consideration, surely they should be at the command of the public. It is of no moment where a man dwells, but it is of immense importance that he be a wise man rather than a fool—a man of integrity rather than a knave.

4thly. Experience, the only save and unerring guide, is altogether in favor of elections at large rather than by Districts. The representation of this State in Congress has ever been of the most respectable character—It is not too much to say that no State in the Union can justly claim a superiority to Connecticut in this respect. The fame may be affirmed, with truth, of the upper house of the Legislature of this State. Has there not been a constant succession of able and wise men in that branch of the administration of Connecticut? For more than a century we have preserved an unexampled prosperity. —shall we hazard our interests on the speculations of zealous partizans who are constantly bewildering themselves and their followers in new schemes?

Another project is that of universal suffrage. The streets resound with the clamour that men are deprived of the invaluable privilege of choosing their rulers, and the people are invited to extend this privilege to all who pay taxes and do military duty. It is now discovered that Connecticut, in this particular, is not free. —The great argument urged in support of universal suffrage is that taxation and representation should go hand in hand—it is said that this maxim was deemed just during the revolutionary war, and that Americans adhered to it as a fundamental principle. —This principle the writer readily recognizes as a sound and indisputable position in every free government. But what is the meaning of the maxim? Does it intend that every person who is taxed, can of right claim the privilege of giving his suffrage? If so persons convicted of offences, or who are infamous for their vices may vote—for such persons are not outlawed. —On this principle, women of full age and unmarried, are also to be admitted. — Minors also whose property is taxed, should be permitted to exercise this franchise, at least by guardian or proxy. What then is the true meaning of the maxim, that representation and taxation are inseparable? Here all writers agree—it means that no community should be taxed by the legislature unless that community is, or might have been represented in such legislature. —Hence several towns in this State till lately, were not represented in the General Assembly, and of course not taxed. — Barkhempsted, Colebrook, and Winchester, it is believed, were of this description.

This State and the other States understood this maxim precisely as now explained, in their opposition to Great-Britain. —We complained that the colonies should not be taxed because they were not represented in parliament. In this view of the subject the maxim is wise and just.

Again, is not every town in Connecticut now represented in the legislature, and of course each individual equally with every other? In the representative of Hartford, for example, a representative of the freemen of Hartford, or of the town of Hartford? The truth is, every man, woman and child are represented.

But it is said that many persons are excluded from giving their suffrages who have life, liberty and reputation to protect. On a close attention to this fact it will be found that the number of those worthy members of society who do not possess the legal qualification, is small, and if men are to have an influence in elections according to the amount of their taxes, why should not the man who pays fifty dollars, be entitled to more than one vote? No one pleads for such a privilege, but there are many who insist that the man without a cent of property shall have the same direction in the choice of those who are charged with the interests of the community, as he who is worth thousands of dollars. A friend to the rights of man seems to feel no alarm at the idea that one who exhausts his earnings in the grog-shop, should have an influence in elections in proportion to strength of his lungs, or his activity in intrigue, but he is greatly agitated from an apprehension that men who have property to protect, will not promote the well being of society. A juror who is to decide on the controversies of his neighbours—an appraiser of land—a distributor of a deceased persons estate, must be freeholders by a standing law which is the subject of no ensure, and yet it is said that in the important transaction of choosing men to enact laws, and to appoint those who are to decide on, and execute those laws, no qualifications are necessary.

Again, it is insisted by those who oppose universal suffrage, and the reader is desired to notice the remark with attention, that no community can be safe unless the power of elections resides principally with the great body of the landholders. Such an influence had this principle on those wise men who formed our laws, that a mere trifle in real property gives the right of suffrage, while a man may be excluded who is the proprietor of personal property to a large amount.

Landholders have an enduring interest in the welfare of the community. They are lords of their own soil, and of course, to a certain degree, independent—they therefore will resist tyranny—they will equally oppose anarchy because they are aware that in any storm which may arise they must abide its fury. The merchant, with his thousands, can seek a shelter—to the mere bird of passage, who has no "abiding country and who seeks none to come, " it is of little moment whether stability or confusion predominate, but to the former who is enchained to the State, peace and order is of inestimable value.

What, my fellow citizens, is the attempt now making? What is the language of those who advocate universal suffrage? It is nothing less than an effort to rest from the farmers of Connecticut that controul over the elections which is their only fortress of safety. Let men who wish to protect their invaluable rights ponder on these things, and let them at the same time, remember that no nation in which universal suffrage hath been allowed, hath remained free and happy.

Another project urged, with great vehemence, is, to displace all our present rulers—by those, is meant our legislators in the general and state Government—our judges and magistrates of every grade. That such is a darling object with those who seek to revolutionize Connecticut, there is no doubt. Is such a measure wise?

Who are these rulers? A candid observer must reply, they are men in whose hands power has been wisely placed by the people, and who have never abused that power, men of unquestionable talents and of spotless fame. Among them are your Trumbulls, your Ellsworths, your Hillhouses, your Griswolds, your Goodriches and your Cavenports, men tried and approved. Among them there is one who was side by side with your beloved Washington during the revolutionary war, who has repeatedly been elected your first magistrate, and, against whom, the tongue of slander never moved but in the hard service of a harder master. There is another, who, for more than twenty years has been employed in the first offices in the gift of his country, and whose probity and talents are second to those of none of his contemporaries. Among these are many who must enjoy the affection and veneration of their countrymen while superior worth is regarded. Against these men the cry is raised—not the cry of the oppressed, for God knows no man in Connecticut is oppressed, but the cry of those who pant for office, and who can rise only on the ruins of others.

Your judges also to whom is committed the administration of justice, are marked out as the victims of party spirit. Is not a wise and faithful execution of the laws the chief object of every good Government? Without this who is safe for a moment? Without this, liberty can exist only in name—The name indeed may be blasphemously uttered, but the substance is gone with the liberty of all who have relied on professions. Let the people of Connecticut look at their tribunals of justice.

Are they not filled with men of incorruptible integrity? Where has innocence received a more ample protection? Is not the transgressor punished, and are not the wrongs of the injured redressed? Are not our mild laws executed in mercy, and is not justice awarded with impartiality to individuals? Can you look at the seat of justice and say "iniquity is there? " Dare any man say that the judges of our high Courts are not upright, intelligent and learned? Who then can justly complain? Yet the stripling of yesterday—the bold projector—the unprincipled ad ambitious, with a host of deceived followers, with matchless effrontery, arraign the conduct of these magistrates and loudly demand that they be driven from their offices, and from public confidence.

Another favorite scheme is to elevate to all the offices of importance men who have never enjoyed the public confidence. The language of these revolutionists is, respecting the men in power in Connecticut, "We will not have these men to rule over us"—We will fill their places with men of our choice—the creatures of our hands, and who will be subservient to our views. But, my countrymen, before you join in this project, pause and enquire, who are these men who thus assert their claim to rule over you? Who are these men who place themselves in the corners of the streets and cry "Oh, that we were made judges in the land? " It is no part of the writer's design to hunt vice from its guilty retreat, to expose before an insulted people, the horrid features which distinguish certain individuals who challenge popular applause, or to attach private character, but justice demands that men who boldly claim to be the rulers of the free and happy state of Connecticut, should be known. The men who are to stand in the places of our Trumbulls and our Ellsworths should not shrink from public investigation. To those who respect the authority of God it is a matter of no small moment that those who rule over men should be just, ruling in the fear of God nor will men, accustomed to revere this solemn declaration, lend their aid to elevate men of vicious and corrupt lives, without some dismay.

It is not enough to tell us that men will be selected of more virtue and talents than those now in power—such a pretence is vain—no man in his senses will regard it—no man makes such a pretence but for wicked purpose. If we are directed to turn our eyes to those who for years past have been held up in the unsuccessful nominations, and are told that these are to be substituted for the men who now guide our Councils, what are we to expect? An appeal may be made to every man not bewildered in this new and destructive madness—he may be asked who among these men stand-forth with fair claims to public confidence? Where among them, can be found the polished scholar—the able civilian, the enlightened judge? Do we see in a single individual an assemblage of talents united with virtue sufficient to qualify him for the seat of justice? If there are such men they have hitherto hid their talents I the earth. It will not here be forgotten that the attempt is, to reject men long known and respected, and to fill their places with those who are without a witness in their favor.

A still more mischievous and alarming project is, that of making a new Constitution for Connecticut. This project originates entirely in a spirit of Jacobinism—it is a new theme on which to descant to effect a revolution in Connecticut. The object is, by false assertions, to induce a belief that no Constitution exists and that tyranny prevails. This party always address the passions and never the understanding. —Review their measures for a few years, and you will distinctly perceive their motives and aims.

To create disaffection and hatred towards those who formerly administered the general Government, it was boldly asserted that the treasury had been plundered. Even the illustrious Saviour of his Country was accused of embezzling public money, and his followers could not expect a less happy fate. Men of the most unsuspected integrity, were openly attacked by anonymous publications, or dispoiled of their good name by secret insinuations. These calumnies were kept in circulation by their authors till impudence itself was abashed, and the object in view obtained—not a tittle of proof was ever adduced, and investigation always shewed that the charges were not only false, but entirely groundless.

For the same unworthy purpose it was asserted in every circle of opposition that salaries were too high, and the incomes of office enormous. Every tavern resounded with this grievance. At length the principal authors of this clamor got into place, and the clamor was hushed. Yes, men who urged the people of Connecticut almost to rebellion on this account, stept into the places and, without a blush, took more from the people than their predecessors. Look at Mr. Babcock's paper in 1799 and 1800, and see its columns filled with railing against high salaries—Look at it since Abraham Bishop takes 3000 dollars a year, and Alexander Wolcott more than four, and find, if you can, a complaint on this subject. Such meanness, such baseness, such hypocrisy in office seekers, exhibit in strong colors the depravity of human nature and teach us what dependence may justly be placed on pretensions and professions.

To inflame the passions and to create animosity, various subjects have been successively seized upon, and pressed into the service of the revolutionists—Every quarrel however trivial is noticed—every seed of discord however small is nourished to disseminate murmurs and to further the great object. -Various classes of the community are told, with apparent anxiety for their welfare, that they are oppressed, and that a new order of things must arise, or that they will be enslaved. New subjects are started as old ones cease to operate, and thus all that ingenuity and art, industry and perseverance, can devise or effect is accomplished. Thus, that numerous and respectably body of Christians called Episcopalians have been told, and repeatedly told, that the more numerous denomination were seeking to deprive them of their just and equal rights, and to subject them to the tyranny of an overbearing majority—These tales were reiterated till their authors found them useless from their folly and falsehood. At another time the Baptists are addressed by a set of men who denied the reality of any religion and the most earnest yearnings for their welfare.

They tyranny of the Legislature was painted in horrid colors, and they were exhorted to lend their aid to vindicate the cause of the oppressed. Those who conscientiously believe that no taxes ought to be paid for the support of religion, and those who wish that religion might no more infest the residence of men, were addressed with considerations adapted to their respective cases. At one time men destitute of property are seduced by the alluring doctrine of universal suffrage—then the farmer is told that taxes are too high on land, and, with the same breath, the mechanic is sagely informed, that the poll tax should be repealed, and the burden fall back on the land holder.

Festivals under the pretence of honoring the election of Mr. Jefferson and Mr. Burr, and of extolling the wisdom of the purchase of Louisiana, but with a real design to blazen the fame of those who assume the character of friends of the people that they may the more readily destroy the most free and equitable Government in the world, are continually holden, and the discontented, the factious, the ambitious and the corrupt, are collected and flattered with declamations in the various shapes of prayers, sermons and orations. Thus a people enjoying the height of political prosperity are cajoled into a belief that men without virtue, without the restraints of the gospel, without a particle of real regard for their fellow men, are their best friends, and are anxiously laboring to promote their good. Let such remember, that when the Ethiopian shall change his skin, when the Leopard shall change his spots, and when bitter fountains shall send forth sweet water, then will those who flatter the people with their tongues, and deceive them with their lips seek their happiness. Such are some of the measures resorted to by those who have sworn in their wrath that Connecticut shall be revolutionized. Finding all these ineffectual, and that the good sence and virtue of Connecticut has hitherto opposed an inseparable barrier to all their plans, they now exclaim Connecticut has no Constitution. Such a gross absurdity could never have been promulgated till the mind was in some degree prepared, by being accustomed to misrepresentation. This was well known to Mr. Bishop, who has for years been in the habit of disregarding moral obligation. In the year 1789 this Orator pronounced several inflammatory invectives against the Constitution of the United States, to which he was a bitter enemy till he obtained an office under it worth three thousand dollars a year. At that time his language was, The Constitution of Connecticut is the best in the world—it has grown up with the people, and is fitted to their condition. —Now this consistent man who is endeavoring to gull the people that he may successfully tyrannize over them, avows that they are without a Constitution.

My fellow citizens, examine this head of clamor with candor, read the solemn declaration of Washington in the title page, attend to the following remarks, and then tell me if you do not perceive in this project, with the manner in which it is supported and attempted to be accomplished, enough of the revolutionary spirit of France, to excite the indignation of every real friend to the peace and happiness of Connecticut.

1. If there be no Constitution in Connecticut then your Huntingtons, your Trumbulls, your Shermans, your Wolcotts and your Davenports, with many other worthies, who were your defence in war, and your ornament in peace, and who are now sleeping with their fathers, were wicked usurpers —they ruled their fellow citizens without authority—they were TYRANTS. Let Judd and Bishop approach the sepulchures of these venerable men—let them lift the covering from these venerable ashes and in the face of heaven pronounce them TYRANTS!! Could you see them approach their dust with such language on their tongues, you would see them retreat with horrible confusion from these relicks of departed worth.

2. The present rulers are acting also without authority, and their laws are void—then you are already in the midst of anarchy and wild misrule —then has no man a title to an inch of land, and you are ready for an equal of division of property—all protection of life and liberty is at an end, and the will of a mob is now to prevail.

3. If indeed there is no Constitution, then the oath which has been administered in your freemen's meetings for twenty years, by which each man has sworn "to be true and faithful to the Constitution" of the state, is worse than impious profanation of the name of God—then your judges, magistrates and jurors have stripped men of their property, condemned some to Newgate and others to the Post, the Pillory and the Gallows without a warrant, and are therefore murderers. —O thou God of order in this our condition!!! But,

4. We have a Constitution—a free and happy Constitution. It was to our fathers like the shadow of a great rock in a weary land—it has enabled them to transmit to us a fair and glorious inheritance—if we suffer revolutionists to rob us of this birth right "then we are bastards and not sons. "

It is a fact as well authenticated as the settlement of the state, that a Constitution was formed by the people of the then colony of Connecticut, before the Charter of King Charles. This Charter was a guarantee of that Constitution. Trumbull's history of Connecticut gives us this Constitution and its origin. On our separation from Great- Britain, the people, thro' their representatives, made the following declaration on this subject:

"An Act containing an Abstract and Declaration of the Rights and Privileges of the People of this State, and securing the same. THE People of this State, being by the Providence of God, free and independent, have the sole and exclusive Right of governing themselves as a free, sovereign, and independent State; and having from their Ancestors derived a free and excellent Constitution of Government whereby the Legislature depends on the free and annual Election of the People, they have the best Security for the Preservation of their civil and religious Rights and Liberties. And forasmuch as the free Fruition of such Liberties and Privileges as Humanity, Civility and Christianity call for, as is due to every Man in his Place and Proportion, without Impeachment and Infringement, hath ever been, and wilt be the Tranquility and Stability of Churches and Commonwealths; and the Denial thereof, the Disturbance, if not the Ruin of both.

PAR. I. BE it enacted and declared by the Governor, and Council and House of Representatives, in General Court assembled: That the ancient Form of Civil Government, contained in the Charter from Charles the Second, King of England, and adopted by the People of this State, shall be and remain the Civil Constitution of this State under the sole authority of the People thereof, independent of any King or Prince whatever. And that this Republic is, and shall forever be and remain, a free, sovereign and independent Sate, by the Name of the STATE of CONNECTICUT.

2. And be it further enacted and declared, That no Man's Land shall be taken away: No Man's Honor or good Name shall be stained: No Man's Person shall be arrested, restrained, banished, dismembered, nor any Ways punished: No Man shall be deprived of his Wife or Children; No Man's Goods or Estate shall be taken away from him nor any Ways indamaged under the Color of Law, or Countenance of Authority; unless clearly warranted by the Laws of this State.

3. That all the Free Inhabitants of this or any other of the United States of America, and Foreigners in Amity with this State, shall enjoy the same justice and Law within this State, which is general for the State in all Cases proper for the Cognizance of the Civil Authority and Court of Judicature within the same, and that without Partiality or Delay.

4. And that no Man's Person shall be restrained, or imprisoned, by any Authority whatsoever, before the Law hat sentenced him thereunto, if he can and will give sufficient Security, Bail, or Mainprize for his Appearance and good Behaviour in the mean Time, unless it be for Capital Crimes, Contempt in open Court, or in such Cases wherein some express Law doth allow of, or order the same. "

These proceedings have been regarded as the ark of our political safety by the great and the good of all parties, who have gone before us. Never till this year have we heard, or even suspected that our state was governed by lawless mobs. Now, as a means to effect a revolution, for the first time, have a few designing men endeavored to excite alarm— they have indeed excited alarm—sober men of their own party are alarmed—honest men, who are not misguided, see the whole extent of this project and they will frown it into contempt.

5. Mr. Edwards, as chairman of a body of men whom he calls a State Committee, on the 30th of July, without consulting even his brethren of the Committee, ordered delegates to meet at New-Haven on the 5th Wednesday of August. In those towns where enough could not be assembled to elect a member, the person written to, was authorized to attend and take a seat. In some towns the proposition was rejected even by Republicans. The delegates thus chosen, with all who united with their opinions, and chose to attend, met at the time and place appointed—shut their doors against every eye and ear— sat one day, formed an address, ordered ten thousand

copies printed and dissolved. This address we have seen. It deserves some notice:

The first thing that attracts our attention is, that William Judd, Esq. of Farmington, is appointed chairman. This was an admirable provision —such a meeting should certainly have such a head. A man with the habit of devoting his feeble talents to intrigue, and who is noticeable only for an ostentatious parade, would preside in such an assembly with peculiar grace. His acquaintance could not but approve of this exhibition of the power of inflammable air and be pleased with its effects [on] an exhausted receiver. The meeting thus organized proceeded to stile this Convention as follows: "AT a meeting of Delegates from ninety-seven towns of the state of Connecticut, convened at New-Haven on the 29th of August, 1804. " Delegates—Delegates do they stile themselves? The people would be obliged to this Convention to disclose their authority. Who commissioned these gentlemen for this important labor of providing them with a Constitution? The truth is not a man in that Convention was chosen by a majority of the people of [their] town—in many instances with less than a quarter part, and in general with less than a tenth— — yet they call themselves Delegates. Thus [the] Convention with Major Judd in the chair, precede their address [with] a grosly deceptive declaration—-a declaration notoriously false and [impu]dent. They then declare it as their unanimous opinion, "that the people of this state are at present without a Constitution of civil Government. " This was to have been expected. Mr. Edwards ordered them to meet for that purpose, and shall they not obey their master? Bishop and Wolcott have repeatedly directed them to make this declaration, and Major Judd knows it to be true. Can any man doubt either the truth of this remark or the sincerity with which it is uttered? Is it not clear that this whole proceeding originates in a pure unmixed affection for the people and a sacred regard to truth? My fellow citizens, look at the whole course of the lives of Judd, (I place him first on the list because he was chairman) of Bishop and of Wolcott, and say if they have not ever been under the influence of the most disinterested virtue and the most exalted patriotism? Look also at these Delegates from ninety-seven towns, and say if they can have any other object in view but the dignity, happiness and glory of their country? Individuals can only vouch for individuals. The writer can vouch for about thirty with Major Judd at their head.

If any reader shall think that the subject is treated with too much levity, he should reflect that we are now animadverting on this Convention in their appointment of chairman, their stiling themselves Delegates from ninety-seven towns, and their declaration that we have no Constitution. On these subjects it is scarcely possible to be serious.

The address proceeds to declare how many of the confederated states have made for themselves Constitutions. We ask, which of them is more prosperous than Connecticut? In which of them are the great interests of Society better secured? In New-York a Convention was called about three years since to amend their Constitution. In Pennsylvania they have had two Constitutions and they are now on the eve of a civil war. Duane the great moving spring of all Jacobin societies, a vile outcast from Europe, reigns with uncontroled sway in every measure, and every man of virtue is denounced.

In Georgia they have had two Constitutions, and in Vermont two, and who dare pronounce their political situation equal to that of Connecticut. The people of France have had six Constitutions within fifteen years, and where are those Constitutions? In the grave of anarchy and despotism with millions of deluded inhabitants who have been sacrificed by the Robespieres and the Bishops of that suffering nation. To that suffering nation turn your eyes and reflect that the mighty mass of woe under which they have groaned, was produced by an ambition, fierce, cruel and destructive as hell, and that an ambition alike terrible reigns every where.

Read this address attentively, and you will be struck with the idea that no grievance is mentioned——not a single evil is pointed out—-indeed the Convention declare that they must be "excused a detail of the numerous wrongs which have arrived to us under this Government"——these are their words—-they are excused indeed—-yes, they are excused from not polluting their address with falsehoods in this particular—-full well they knew that no such wrongs existed——full well they anticipated that a certain detection would follow any such attempt at imposition. The leaders in this Convention knew full well that there is intelligence enough in Connecticut to meet them on any complaint, and to shew that it is groundless.

They, therefore, prudently decline to be explicit, and yielding to us that the Government is now well administered, they shew a great anxiety for the safety of the "next generation. " What an astonishing display of philanthropy!! Bishop and Wolcott are not at ease in their hearts while there is a prospect that even the generations which succeed us, will experience a woe!!

After many remarks directed to the passions, without proposing in specific terms a single provision of their newly projected Constitution, without laying their finger upon a single grievance, without urging a single argument tending to shew that a Constitution does not exist, the address unmakes itself—-it unmasks the Convention—-it unmasks these patriotic Delegates, and discovers the true cause of this Jacobinic meeting. Towards the close of it, speaking of the people, it says, "By their votes will be known their decision. If a Constitution appears desirable, they will vote for men who are in favor of it. " Here the Convention speak which all may understand—-but lest they had not made themselves sufficiently intelligible, they add, "We ask men of all parties to attend punctually at proxies and to continue a contest of votes till the great question whether this state shall have a Constitution be settled finally and forever. " Now, the plain English of these sentences is this "We who are here assembled in Convention wish the people of Connecticut to vote for such men, in future, for office, as are in favor of a new Constitution—-we have already declared that we are in favor of such a Constitution—-pray therefore vote for us and continue" the context "till we succeed and then"—-yes—-my fellow- citizens, and then, what will they do? Why laugh at your folly—-take all the offices and leave you to take care of yourselves. IF such would not be their conduct then the sun will no more rise in the east.

Gentlemen of the convention pray cease your pretensions to promotion till the people discover your merit. If you are honest, great and wise you will certainly be noticed and promoted—if you are pygmy politicians, the mushroom growth of an hour, dressed only with the little brief authority of self created delegates to a self created convention to aggrandise yourselves, then probably you will live with little further notice, and it will only be said hereafter of you that you belonged to an assembly convened at New-Haven on the 29th of August 1804, which sprang up in a day, chose major Judd chairman; and like "Jonah's Gourd withered in a day. "

In this convention the question was much discussed whether the address should be made to the people or to the constituted authority of our State, the legislature. Some honest republicans insisted that it was proper to apply to the Legislature, but this was opposed by the young lawyers and the leaders of the party universally— full well they knew that such a measure would not answer their purpose—Mobs never talk of any authority except that of the sovereign people—To the sovereign people they go, and to the sovereign people they appeal till a sovereign people are cruelly insulted, cajoled and enslaved. Marat, Robespierre and Bonaparte told the sovereign people that they were all in all till they had robbed them of their dearest interests, and enchained them in despotism, and they now mock them with such declarations as these, * "The perfectability of human nature, the worst disease of man"-"the caprice of elections must be destroyed"-"the people cannot govern themselves"

Having examined some of the plans or projects proposed for our adoption, we will now estimate the probably cost attending them. It is to be recollected that the proposition is to change the vital principles of our government—to displace our present rulers and to fill their places with men who never enjoyed the public confidence. To determine whether these objects are worth accomplishing, it is necessary to COUNT THE COST.

1. One part of this cost will be an increase of the violence of parties. Men who regard their property, their liberty and their lives, will not yield them a willing sacrifice to the demands of the ambitious and unprincipled—men who faced danger and braved death during a seven years war—men whose veins are warm with the blood of their venerable ancestors who planted this happy state, and defended it amidst innumerable hardships and calamities—men who deem their birthright sacred—their own freedom valuable, and their children dear as their own blood, will not calmly, nor cowardly suffer those who have no claims but their impudence, to storm their fortress and to capture them. They will defend it in all lawful ways. -Bishop and Wolcott, and a thousand other mercenary hirelings may attempt to subdue or terrify them—a proud and haughty leader who under the guise of patriotism, is attempting to undermine the happiness

of the best regulated and freest State in the Union, with a thousand sycophants, conspiring to bring us under the yoke of Virginia, may exhaust their ingenuity and malice, still Connecticut will remain unshaken. She will never crouch like Isachar to chains and fetters while any portion of the noble spirit of her ancestors who transmitted this fair inheritance at a mighty expense, remains to impel them to noble exertions. —It is ardently to be wished that the passions of those who seek to overturn the venerable institutions of Connecticut, my subside, and that a spirit of reconciliation and moderation may succeed to that madness which threatens our peace. —If however the controversy is to be continued and a mob insist on the right to rule, freemen will protect their lives and their liberties. —And is not the peace and tranquility of the State of importance? We have been told with more truth than sincerity that "life itself is a dreary thing" without "harmony in social intercourse. " Happy would it have been if the author of that just and pertinent remark had not contributed more than any other man in the United States to embitter parties, and to render life indeed a "dreary thing. "

2. Another item in the expense of accomplishing these projects, is a corruption of morals. To revolutionize Connecticut it will be necessary to circulate, without any intermission, many gross falsehoods respecting the men in power, the judges, legislators and magistrates, and the acts and proceedings of the General Assembly. We have seen the columns of the Mercury and the Republican Farmer filled with vile libels. —WE have seen Abraham Bishop followed by hundreds enter a temple devoted to

the service of God, and we have heard him there utter the most malignant slanders on the Clergy, the Legislature and the Courts of law. —We have seen him publicly denounce one class and another of his fellow citizens as hypocrites, old tories and traitors. —We have seen him receiving for this, the applause of a wretched collection of disappointed, ambitious and corrupt men. This has been borne and the author despised, and indignantly hissed from the society of the respectable and virtuous—but the end is not gained—new themes of reviling—new subjects of abuse must be sought, and the party who wish to effect a revolution, are pledged to uphold and protect the agents however wicked. What then may now be expected? That dreadful declaration "Truth is fallen in their streets" will soon be but an inconsiderable part of our miserable character. It need not be added that such a condition evinces great corruption of morals.

3. Another part of this expense will be the elevation of men to office who are unworthy of public confidence. What can a nation or state expect from such men? What could now be expected from these men but that they become immediately the creatures of a party—the tools of a faction? Is it worthy of no consideration that judges who are to be the arbiters of controversies—who are to adjudicate on the lives of their fellow citizens, and to whom is committed the dearest and highest interests of society, should be men of virtue—of wisdom and of unsullied reputation? Can a Court be a shield against the proud oppressor when a daring leader can crush them with his nod? Be not deceived my fellow citizens—no nation hath yet made such an experiment without feeling

its bitter and dreadful effects. See the revolutionary tribunals of France—See in them a melancholy picture of corrupt courts and unprincipled judges—The cruelty of that nation hath appeared no where more infernal than through their forms of law and in their sanctuaries of justice—a corrupt judgment seat is the greatest curse with which a people can be punished. In the mean time all subordinate tribunals will partake of the same character. —Thus instead of a government of laws, there will be the tyranny of a desperate faction. —Let no one reply that there is no danger of such evils in Connecticut. We now see a few leaders controul a party of several thousands—We have seen six hundred meet and applaud the purchase of Louisiana when not one in five of them could form any opinion on the merits of the bargain—WE have seen a few leaders direct the offering of incense to Burr while the great body of their followers cursed him—We see a party suffering the pride of Virginia to controul the government of the Union and to oppress New-England with a heavy impost because she would not submit to internal taxes—We see a few leaders direct a convention of about two hundred to issue an address to the people of Connecticut, which address contains on the face of it many palpable falsehoods. — And cannot these same leaders controul a Court?

4. Another part of the cost of these projects, is the loss of all our institutions of religion. —It is not here intended that these institutions will be at once abolished—Such a measure would alarm some honest men of the party—a gradual but sure destruction is the evil to be feared. The constitution of the United States was first attacked by an

unconstitutional repeal of a law, and now the independence of the Supreme Court is to be destroyed, by impeachments of the judges. So will it fare with your institutions. The principle openly advocated is that none shall be obliged to contribute for the support of religious institutions. This once established destroys the vitals of the system, and the residue of its existence will be misery and wretchedness. Shall a party avowing this sentiment and seeking by every artifice to give it effect, receive the support of a people who have derived such substantial benefits from these institutions? Shall we look in vain thro' the ranks of that party for one to lift up his voice against this daring and dangerous innovation? Are there not many who either do not believe this to be the object of their leaders, or if such shall be their object, who are determined to resist them? Yes, there are many who act with them, who still intend to progress to no such excesses. Let such view the conduct of similar parties— Let such not be deceived—This is indeed their object— They do not avow it to you, they know you would reject it, but they have made a vow that the influence of the Clergy shall be destroyed—this can be done in no other way. Nor can you resist them—they regard you now because they wish your assistance to confer on them power, but will they regard you when your exertions can neither aid nor defeat their designs? —surely not—such has been the conduct of all factions. —It will be theirs should they prevail—The world has not furnished one solitary exception, nor can you expect one in this case. They seek their own good, and not the good of others, if inspiration is to be credited.

In return for these losses what good is to acrue to the people? Will you hazard these evils without a fair and reasonable expectation of some solid benefits? Is it then unreasonable to enquire what good is to be obtained? Do the characters of these men elevate your hopes? You know many of them in private life—do they there abound in good works? Shall they be heard and regarded when they demand of you to displace your faithful and approved rulers, and commit to them your all? Modest men will wait your notice and rise at your request. Shall the impudent, banish them from your affections and usurp their places in your hearts?

Let it again be asked what good will result to Connecticut by a new Constitution, by the prevalence of revolutionary principles? France, Switzerland, the Netherlands, Italy and Holland, have seen revolution after revolution, one new Constitution after another, and liberty has a thousand times been immovably established. Altars have been demolished —Temples polluted, Kings, Queens, Nobles and Priests murdered in the cause of liberty—millions have perished—religion banished, and the worship of God prohibited—projectors have exhausted their ingenuity —the treasures of wealth have been wasted and the peace of the world sacrificed! What is the result? An accumulation of misery which baffles all description. Not an individual is more happy or more virtuous. Not a nation more prosperous—not a tittle added to human felicity. Ye reformers, look at France—behold the crimes which have risen up to demand the vengeance of God—see the woes which you have brought on the race of man, and tremble lest your works should follow you?

If this picture is too glaring, look at our sister states in which revolutions have been effected, and shew us the benefit. A noisy or seditious individual has obtained a lucrative office—an ambitious leader is in the char of state satiating his pride, or like Abraham Bishop gratifying his passion for ignoble pelf, upon his thousands. —He drives his carriage by his industrious neighbor who has toiled for him at an election, cracks his whip, and laughs at the folly of his dupe, and will laugh till he may need his services again, and then he will again cringe and bow and flatter and gull. But is the mechanic, the farmer, the merchant profited? Is society enriched, or the public good promoted?

In this view of the subject we will briefly ask, in the third place, is it proper to make the proposed changes—to adopt these projects? If no benefits will result—if much evil will probably ensue—the course of duty and interest is plain. Aware, however, that it may be said many of the dangers are imaginary, and are founded upon the supposition that we shall act with as little discretion and prudence as the people of other countries, it is important to observe that revolutions are the same, in nature in every nation. Those who speak of a new Constitution, and of thorough reforms, should recollect that the promoters of these schemes in France, constantly amused the people with the idea that a new order of things—new rights—new principles, were to arise. Who does not recollect to have read of the perfectability human nature—of the enlightened age of regenerated France? She boldly proclaimed herself the example of the world, and all nations were invited to see her glory, and enjoy her blessed liberty and her glorious equality. But mark the issue —Not twelve years have elapsed before she has returned to an inglorious despotism—She has exchanged her Capets for a foreign usurper, with an incalculable loss, and here her history ends. Such is the constant termination of such revolutions, and shall we claim to be an exception? How do we judge as to the propriety of any course of life except by observation, experience or history? We see industry and integrity rewarded with competence or wealth—we see intemperance and sloth followed with disease, loss of reputation and poverty. These are sure grounds on which to predict respecting our neighbors, and by which to regulate our own conduct. On similar principles a wise people regard the conduct of other nations, and are solemnly admonished by their example. Let not then the projector persuade us to adopt his theories with proofs of their danger thus glaring before our eyes. Look at the conduct of our revolutionists for four years past, and see if you do not discover the genuine principles of the Jacobins of France—Recollect also that they had first a Convention— then an Executive Directory—then a Consul for years— then a Consul for life, and then an usurper with an hereditary descent in his family. At each successive revolution the people were courted—were flattered— were promised transcendent felicity. The people swore eternal hatred to Monarchy, and eternal fidelity to Constitutions, till, heaven, weary of their perjuries, sent them a despot in his wrath.

My fellow citizens human nature is the same here as in France—Then before you give ear to the songs of enchantment Count the Cost—Before you sell your birthright for a mess of pottage Count the Cost. Before you consent to yield up the institutions of your wise and pious ancestors, Count the Cost—Before you admit universal suffrage Count the Cost—Before you submit to the mischievous doctrine of district elections, Count the Cost. —Before you reject from office the men whom your hearts approve, Count the Cost, the great cost of weak and wicked rulers. —Before you consent to be governed by men whose impudence, and vice constitute many of their claims to promotion, Count the Cost. This evil you can prevent by attending with punctuality on our elections. The freemen of Connecticut are mighty when they arise in their strength. No freeman can justify absence except from necessity. —That people who will not faithfully attend upon the Choice of their rulers, cannot expect to retain their freedom. —Trust not to a majority—say not that things will go well without me— Such language is unbecoming freemen—Despair not of a majority—if you will not "go with the multitude to do evil, " go against them to do good. Before you neglect an election Count the Cost —If the loss of your Vote should prove the loss of an election of a single man, then will you not have Counted the Cost.

My fellow citizens—WE have a government which has protected us a Century and an half—we have enjoyed unexampled prosperity. —WE may transmit a glorious inheritance to posterity. —The writer has children dear to him as his own blood—these children are to him a sacred deposit—He can, with confidence, commit their political interests to such a government as Connecticut has enjoyed. —He is persuaded that if they feel the iron hand of despotism, it will not be from such a government, and such rulers as we now possess—Before he yields his own, and their dear, and inestimable rights to the wild projects of the reformers of this age, he is firmly resolved to sit down and Count the Cost, and he entreats his fellow citizens to adopt similar resolutions.

APPENDIX.

A View of the Fiscal Concerns of Connecticut.

Capital Funds of the Civil List.

	Dols.	Cts.
Funded 6 per cent. Stock, (real capital) -	209,273	83
Deferred —do. - do. - do. - -	148,632	83
Funded 3 per cent. do. - - -	50,038	11
Bank Stock - - - - -	44,725	
	425,669	77

School Funds.

	Dols.	Cts.
Bonds collaterally secured - -	1,020,542	27
New Lands received in payment of School Bonds, price at which received,	194,000	
Funded 6 per cent. Stock, (real capital)	14,048	
Deferred —do. - do. -do. - - -	5,455	7
Funded 3 per cent. do. - - -	4,570	95
	1,238,617	29

Annual Expense of Government. Viz.

Salaries of Executive Officers, - -	8,630
Debentures and Contingent expenses of the Legislature for two Sessions, -	17,100
Debenture of the Supreme Court of Errors,	550
Judicial expenses, - - - -	6,100
Expense of Newgate prison, - - -	4,000
Charges of Paupers and Vagrants, - -	4,500
Allowance of 2 dollars on the 1000 of the list being a draw-back from the State Tax,	12,000
Contingent Expenses, comprising all other charges of Government, - - -	6,200
	59,080

Means for defraying the annual expense of the Civil List.
  Viz.
Annual Interest on the above-mentioned Stock
  appertaining to the Civil List Funds,   26,553   54
Duties on Civil Processes,   -   -   5,700
Annual Tax of 7 Mills on the Dollar,
  neat amount,   -   35,700
                                               —————————
                                               67,953   54

N. B. One eighth part of all the State taxes and one tenth part of all rateable polls are abated for the relief of the indigent.

The yearly Interest of the whole School Funds
  would be -   74,179   88
Deduct the Interest on that part which lies
in lands, and also on those Bonds whereon
Interest has not yet commenced, amounts to   7, 324   12

N.B. Several Bonds draw Interest in present year, which were not on Interest last year.

And the whole present annual Interest will be 66,855   76
Add to this the allowance of
2 dolls. On the 1000 of the List,   -   - 12,000

Total annual amount payable for schools,   78,855   76

Drawable from the State Treasury annually,
by the people in their capacity of
School Societies,   -   78,855   76

Payable by the people into the State Treasury
  annually in taxes (including duties on
  civil processes) only the sum of   -   41,400

Balance drawn out beyond what is paid by
  taxes and duties,   -   -   -   -   37,455   76

From the foregoing view of their financial arrangements, it appears that the people of Connecticut not only enjoy the blessings of Civil Government free from expense, but even receive from the public Treasury yearly, in sum of 37,455 dollars and 76 cents more than they contribute to in taxes, &c.

Who can behold this uparalleled situation of finances, taking into view at the same time our embarrassed circumstances at the close of the late war, when we were not only destitute of any funds except direct taxes, but incumbered with a debt of two millions of Dollars, and not admire and appreciate the faithfulness and ability of those who have so sucessfully managed the public affairs of this State.